Cambridge English Readers

Starter Level

Series editor: Philip Prowse

Why?

Philip Prowse

T0094913

CAMBRIDGE
UNIVERSITY PRESS

University Printing House, Cambridge CB2 8BS, United Kingdom

One Liberty Plaza, 20th Floor, New York, NY 10006, USA

477 Williamstown Road, Port Melbourne, VIC 3207, Australia

314–321, 3rd Floor, Plot 3, Splendor Forum, Jasola District Centre, New Delhi – 110025, India

79 Anson Road, #06–04/06, Singapore 079906

Cambridge University Press is part of the University of Cambridge.

It furthers the University's mission by disseminating knowledge in the pursuit of
education, learning and research at the highest international levels of excellence.

www.cambridge.org
Information on this title: www.cambridge.org/9780521732956

First published 2008
Reprinted 2019

Philip Prowse has asserted his right to be identified as the Author of the Work in
accordance with the Copyright, Design and Patents Act 1988.

Printed in the United Kingdom by Hobbs the Printers Ltd

Illustrations by Paul Dickinson

A catalogue record of this book is available from the British Library.

ISBN-13 978-0-521-73295-6 paperback

Contents

People in the story

Alex is a soldier in the army.

Sara is Alex's girlfriend.

Sergeant Ken is in the army with Alex.

Ada lives in Glossia.

Stefan is a soldier.

Marina and **Happy** are Ada's children.

Hawk is a soldier.

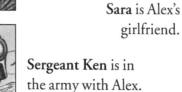

There is no town called Tonek, and no country called Glossia. But there are countries like Glossia all over the world.

Chapter 1   *Goodbye*

'Please don't go to Glossia,' says Sara. 'You're only nineteen.'

Alex is saying goodbye to Sara, his girlfriend.

'I must,' answers Alex. 'I'm a soldier – it's my job. I must go where the army says.'

'But why are you going there?' asks Sara.

'We're going to stop the fighting,' says Alex. 'Lots of people are dying.'

'But why are they fighting?' asks Sara.

'I don't know,' answers Alex.

'Why don't you ask?' says Sara. 'You never ask questions.'

'I know,' answers Alex. 'I'm sorry. I hate asking questions.'

'Please change, Alex,' says Sara. 'For me.'

'I'm going to think about you every day,' says Sara.

'Me too,' Alex answers. 'I can send you a text from my phone tomorrow. And I think there's email.'

'That's good,' Sara says with a little smile. 'I love you, Alex.'

'And I love you too,' answers Alex. 'Now, don't be sad.'

Chapter 2   *We're in Glossia now*

Alex is on the plane to Glossia. He's sitting next to Sergeant Ken. It's Ken's second time in Glossia.

'Excuse me, Sergeant,' Alex starts.

'You can call me Ken,' the sergeant says.

'Why are they fighting in Glossia?' Alex asks.

'That's not an easy question,' Ken answers. 'I think it's like this. Some people have guns. They use the guns because they want something. Then other people get guns to fight back with. Now everyone has guns. And everyone forgets what they are fighting about.'

'But where do the guns come from?' is Alex's next question.

'People from other countries sell them to the Glossians,' Ken answers.

'Why?' asks Alex.

Ken smiles. 'Money, that's why.'

'Ken, can we stop people buying and selling guns?' Alex asks.

'No, we can't. The people who sell the guns – they're thousands of kilometres away. All we can do is help the people here in this country,' answers Ken. 'We're going to a famous old town called Tonek. In Tonek lots of people are fighting each other. And some of them are also fighting us!'

There's a very loud noise, and the plane goes over to the right.

'What's that?' shouts Alex.

'What do you think?' answers Ken. 'We're in Glossia now.'

'Is it always like this?' Alex asks.

'Yes,' Ken answers.

'But the papers say the Glossian people want us here,' Alex says. The sergeant smiles.

'Some Glossians do and some don't,' answers Ken. 'But we're here to help all the people.'

'And is it always hot?' asks Alex.

'Yes,' laughs Ken.

Chapter 3 *SOLDIERS GET OUT!*

Sergeant Ken and Alex drive into Tonek. People watch them.

'Alex, this is where you're living for the next six months,' says Ken. 'Your bed's over there. And this is Hawk.'

A tall man with very short hair stands up and puts out his hand. 'Hi,' he says.

'And that's Stefan on the bed,' Ken says.

Stefan smiles at Alex. 'Hello! Put your things down,' he says. 'Do you want something to eat or drink?'

'Yes, please,' answers Alex.

'I'm going now,' Ken says. 'You must be tired, Alex. Try and get some sleep tonight. We start work in the morning.'

Chapter 4 *First patrol*

The next day it's time for Alex's first patrol.

'Just do what I do,' Ken tells Alex. 'Stefan and Hawk are going to walk behind us. Use your eyes and ears and look everywhere. And don't forget – we never know who is a friend and who isn't.'

'What are we looking for?' asks Alex.

'Guns,' answers Ken with a quick laugh.

'And gunmen,' Hawk says. He isn't laughing.

'But what about the people who sell the guns?' Alex asks.

'They're not here,' Hawk answers. 'They're far away, with their money.'

Some people are happy to see the soldiers. They stop and say hello. But some boys aren't happy that the soldiers are there. They're throwing things at the patrol and shouting. The soldiers don't understand what the boys are shouting.

Something hits Alex in the mouth. He turns with his gun. Alex isn't slow, but the boys are very fast. They run away. Alex feels his mouth.

'Are you OK?' Stefan shouts.

'Yes,' answers Alex.

Then they hear a gun. Someone's shooting at them.

Alex looks across the dirty street at a house. He sees someone at a bedroom window.

'Look! Up there!' Alex shouts.

Hawk turns, looks up and shoots at the window. Ken and Alex run across the street to the house. They open the front door and run up to the bedroom. Hawk and Stefan wait in the street.

email

!	@	⊡	From ▶	Subject	Received

Hi Sara

What a bad day! My first patrol. There's shooting and I see someone at a bedroom window. Hawk shoots at the window. Then Ken and I run into the house and up to the bedroom. But there isn't a gunman there. It's a little boy! The boy's mother comes and shouts at us. I don't understand what she's saying. But I can see she's very angry. I want to say sorry, but I don't speak Glossian. When we leave the woman is shouting and the small boy is crying. I don't feel well. It's all wrong. What am I doing here?

All my love
Alex

Chapter 5 *We have no names*

The next day Sergeant Ken, Alex, Hawk and Stefan are on patrol again. It's twelve o'clock.

A kilometre away a family is finishing lunch. There's a twelve-year-old boy called Happy and an eight-year-old girl called Marina. Their mother's name is Ada and she's very beautiful. There's no father – he's dead.

In the afternoon Ada puts away the lunch things and makes coffee. Happy is sitting on the floor in the living room with Marina. The brother and sister are laughing and playing with a doll. Ada doesn't hear the back door.

Two men come in. One is tall and one is short. The short man has a bag. They're wearing white T-shirts and black trousers. And they have black masks.

Ada looks at the two men. Then she shouts to her children, 'Come here now!' Happy and Marina run to their mother and stand by her. They're afraid of the two men in masks.

'Who are you?' Ada asks the men. They don't answer. The short man puts the bag down and the tall man looks at Ada.

'What are your names?' asks Ada.

'We have no names and we have no faces,' answers the tall man.

'We're not rich. What do you want?' asks Ada.

'Nothing,' answers the short man. 'All we want is your house for ten minutes.'

Chapter 6 *Don't ask stupid questions*

A young woman with a baby comes in the front door.

'Who's she?' asks Ada.

'Ssh!' says the tall man. 'The baby!'

The young woman takes up the baby. It's sleeping. Under the baby is a long gun. The tall man takes the gun and the woman puts the baby down again.

'What are you going to do?' asks Happy.

'A soldier's going to die,' answers the short man.

'Why?' asks Happy.

'Don't ask stupid questions,' says the tall man. 'This is our country. We don't want soldiers from other countries here.'

'You!' the short man shouts to Marina. 'Give me your doll!'

'Do it,' Ada tells her daughter.

Marina gives the man her doll. He takes something out of his bag and puts it in the doll. Then he takes a phone and puts it in the doll too.

'Listen, you two,' the short man tells the children. 'You mustn't play with the doll now. Do you understand?'

'Yes,' Happy answers.

'Here,' the short man says to the young woman with the baby. 'Take the doll and leave it in the street in front of the house.'

The short man speaks to the children. 'Go and play in front of the house now. But when you see the soldiers you must run in again.' He looks at Ada. 'Then you take your children out of the house by the back door. Do you understand?'

'Yes,' says Ada. 'Happy and Marina! Go out and play in the street now. But don't go near the doll!'

The short man gives a phone to the tall man. 'This phone's for you and there's a phone in the doll,' he says.

The tall man takes the gun and the phone up to the
bedroom. The young woman goes with him. Out of the
window they can see the children in the street. And the doll.
The tall man has the phone in his hand.

'All we can do now is wait,' he tells the woman.

'Listen! What's that?' asks the woman. 'Can you hear
something?'

'Yes,' the tall man answers. 'It's the soldiers. They're coming.'

Chapter 7 *They're afraid of us*

'Why are the children running away?' Alex asks Hawk.

'Because they're afraid of us,' Hawk answers.

'But why?' asks Alex. 'We're here to help. Don't they know that we're their friends?'

The patrol gets near to Ada's house.

'Yes, the children must be afraid of us,' Alex says to Hawk. 'Look! That's their doll in the street. I'm going to give it to them. Then they can see we're their friends.'

Alex runs over to the doll.

'Stop!' shouts Ken.

Alex looks up. 'Why?' he asks. 'I'm just trying to help.'

'Do what I say!' shouts Ken. 'Come here now!'

Up in the bedroom, the tall man speaks to the young woman. 'The phone isn't working.' He's very angry.

'What about the gun?' the young woman asks.

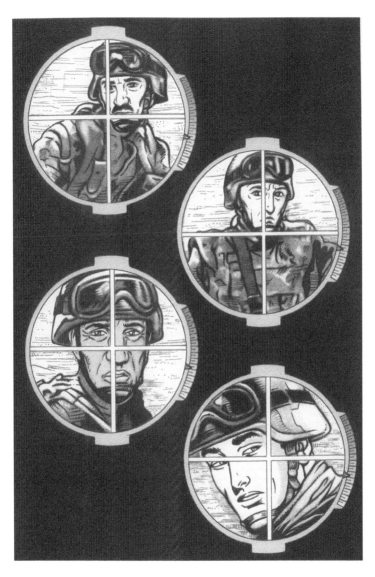

The tall man looks at Hawk, then at Stefan. Then Sergeant Ken. Then he looks at Alex and chooses.

'You're going to die,' he says.

The tall man shoots. Alex's mouth opens and he tries to say something. Then his eyes close. He doesn't say anything. He doesn't see anything. He doesn't feel anything. He's dead.

Hawk turns and looks up. He sees someone at the bedroom window.

'Up there!' Hawk shouts and shoots. Then Ken and Stefan shoot at the window.

The young woman helps the tall man down to the living room.

'Here! Quick! Take the gun!' he says to the young woman. She takes the gun and puts it under the baby.

'Come on! The soldiers are coming!' shouts the short man. 'You must see a doctor.'

'I can't go anywhere,' the tall man says. 'You two go! Now!' He closes his eyes.

Chapter 8 *Don't say anything*

The young woman and the short man run out of the back of the house. Ada and the children are waiting there.

'Where's your friend?' Ada asks.

'Dead,' the young woman answers.

'Why?' asks Happy.

'Because of the soldiers,' the young woman says. She turns and walks away fast with the baby.

'I hate soldiers,' Happy says.

'Don't tell the soldiers about us,' the short man tells Ada. He takes off his mask and she can see his face now. 'And your boy's coming with me. Don't say anything to the soldiers or he dies.' He takes Happy's hand and starts to run off.

'No!' shouts Ada. 'Don't take him! Happy!'

Ken, Hawk and Stefan run in the front door of the house. They see the dead man in the living room. Stefan runs up to the bedroom. Hawk and Ken go out to the back of the house. They find Ada and Marina there.

Hawk speaks a little Glossian. 'Where are they?' he shouts. Ada says nothing.

Then Hawk sees two people running away – a man and a boy. Hawk doesn't wait. He shoots.

'No!' Ada shouts.

Ken takes Ada and Marina into the house.

Half an hour later, two kilometres away, the young woman is walking with the baby. Two soldiers see her and ask her to stop.

'Where are you going?' asks one of the soldiers.

'To the shops,' answers the woman. 'I'm going to buy some food.' She smiles at the soldiers.

'What's in there?' the soldier shouts.

'My baby,' the woman says. 'Please don't shout. He's sleeping.' She smiles again.

'OK, you can go,' says one of the soldiers and smiles at her.

Chapter 9   *Why?*

There are lots of soldiers at Ada's house now. They take Alex and the tall man away in a car. A Glossian man is helping Sergeant Ken. He's asking Ada lots of questions. But Ada doesn't answer. All she can think of is Happy. Where is he? Is he dead? She takes Marina's hand and listens to the questions. But she doesn't answer.

The soldiers leave Ada and Marina in the house. That evening Ada hears a noise at the back door. It's dark. She opens the door and sees Happy there.

'Are the soldiers here?' asks Happy.

'No,' Ada says with a big smile and takes Happy in her arms.

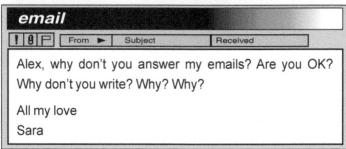

email

| | | From ► | Subject | Received |

Alex, why don't you answer my emails? Are you OK? Why don't you write? Why? Why?

All my love
Sara